IN THE SHADOW OF SAINTS

Sufi Discourses
of
Shaykh Muhammad Hisham Kabbani

Edited by
Dr. Hedieh Mirahmadi

Published by
WORDE
World Organization for Resource Development and Education

© Copyright 2005 by the World Organization for Resource Development and Education. All rights reserved.

No part of this book may be reproduced, stored in a retrieval system, or transmitted in any form, or by any means, electronic, mechanical, photocopying, or otherwise, without the written permission of the World Organization for Resource Development and Education.

Library of Congress Cataloging-in-Publication Data
Kabbani, Muhammad Hisham.
In the shadow of saints : Sufi discourses of Shaykh Muhammad Hisham Kabbani / edited by Hedieh Mirahmadi
p. cm.
ISBN 1-930409-32-X
1. Sufism. 2. Naqshabandīyah
BP189 .K25 2005
297.4 22
2005037954

Published and Distributed by:
WORDE (World Organization for Resource Development and Education)
4200 Wisconsin Ave. NW #106-339
Washington, DC 20016
Tel: (202) 595-1355 Fax: (202) 318-2582
Email: staff @worde.org
Web: http://www.worde.org

Cover design "Saintly Aurora" by Jehan Ali

Shaykh Muhammad Nazim Adil al-Haqqani (lower right), world leader of the Naqshbandi-Haqqani Sufi Order, pictured with Shaykh Muhammad Hisham Kabbani, deputy leader of the Order. These two Sufi masters hold the respect and love of millions around the world.

Acknowledgements

We never could have quenched our thirst for spiritual enlightenment without the fountain of Divine guidance and inspiration that gushes forth from His Holiness Mawlana Shaykh Nazim Adil al-Haqqani. We owe him an eternity of gratitude for taking us from the "darkness into the light." We are especially grateful that he graced us with his beloved student and deputy, Shaykh Muhammad Hisham Kabbani, as a living example of Sufi chivalry, from whom we could learn and aspire to emulate.

Our profound gratitude also goes out to Hajjah Naziha Adil Kabbani for her boundless patience and selfless generosity. We also would like to thank the countless hours of editing and refinement done by the other students, especially Mateen Siddiqui and Ruhi Shamim, as well as the cover design provided by Jehan Ali. We dedicate this book in loving memory of our holy mother, Hajjah Amina Adil. She was the perfect example of spirituality, devotion, and kindness. Her presence is dearly missed.

About Shaykh Kabbani

Shaykh Kabbani hails from a long line of illustrious religious figures. He was born in Beirut, Lebanon, where he began his study of traditional Islamic theology and spirituality. By 18, he could debate complex legal issues with scholars thrice his age. Shaykh Kabbani also studied medicine in Belgium, but he soon discovered that mystical Sufi teachings, what he refers to as "the sweet side of Islam," was his true calling.

For more than 45 years, Shaykh Kabbani has devoted himself to rigorous spiritual training under two eminent Sufi masters: Shaykh Abd Allah ad-Daghestani and Shaykh Nazim Adil al-Haqqani. This has endowed him with the sublime qualities of wisdom, light, intelligence, and the compassion of a true master on the Path. Blessed with these noble qualities, he has brought the diverse spectrum of religions and spiritual paths into harmony, through the recognition of humanity's role as caretaker of one another, and of this fragile planet.

Shaykh Kabbani is respected around the world, by statesmen, academics, and religious leaders who acknowledge him as a holy man, tirelessly committed to the spread of peace, justice, and equality for all. He often leaves the comfort of his tranquil home in the Mid West for the ardors of repeated travel just to inspire seekers wherever he finds them. He is generous with his time, knowledge, and unconditional love—always giving to others selflessly and never revealing the power of his true majesty.

His master, Shaykh Muhammad Nazim Adil al-Haqqani says he is known in the heavenly realm, in the secret circle of

In the Shadow of Saints

Saints, as 'Madad al-Haqq' or 'Supporter of The Truth.' It is not sufficient to introduce him by the fine institutes that he has established from East to West for the last thirty five years across six continents. It is not sufficient to mention the number of years he has been with his Masters GrandShaykh Abd Allah ad-Daghestani and Mawlana Shaykh Muhammad Nazim Adil al-Haqqani. Our minds can't perceive his greatness; our hearts can't hold the love that he deserves from his students. Our eyes can't shed enough tears of love, joy and gratitude for what he gives every moment to humanity across the universe. How do you measure the greatness of such holy people? ❧

Introduction

In a world filled with random violence, terrorism, corruption and human suffering, it is hard to believe that miracles still occur. Yet, if you are fortunate, God will bring you across people that remind you His Divine grace is all around us.

In the mystic tradition of Sufism, we use the term "friend of God"[1] to describe a Saint who has the Divine support of God, including the ability to perform miracles. The person can still be living to be a friend of God and in fact we believe there are always 124,000 living Saints on earth to remind people of God's message to humanity.

I have had the tremendous good fortune of meeting and accompanying one of the world's living Saints, Mawlana Shaykh Muhammad Hisham Kabbani. He travels the world tirelessly—forever changing people's lives and teaching them the love of God. If you ask him, he would never accept the title of Saint, but his humility is one of the qualities that make him so remarkable.

This is a memoir of Shaykh Hisham's talks to students around the world, which introduces you to the Heavenly wisdom and guidance he provides. It includes small anecdotes of advice he gave along the way, which many people should find useful in everyday life.

Sufi's believe that talks given by a real Guide are living words so that if you leave them as originally spoken by the Shaykh, the reader can personally experience that lecture and extract more

---

[1] In Arabic it is *Awliya*.

wisdom than may be written on the page. That is why in some cases, there is background information provided about the circumstances surrounding that talk, in an effort to transport the reader back to that moment in time. For this same reason, I have also not perfected the English grammar style so it maintains the original tone of Shaykh Kabbani.

In order to make the material more accessible to non-Muslim readers, however, most Arabic terminology was replaced with an English translation. For our Muslim readers, I apologize for what is often an over simplification. Where the Arabic word preserves the tone of the talk or is a word used throughout the book, it has been left as is and will be explained in the footnotes.

Since this is a personal account of Shaykh Hisham's lectures, rather than his own publication, any errors you find in substance or form, are my fault and I apologize. I welcome your comments or editorial remarks.

The Shaykh teaches us that sound waves are energy that is never altered or destroyed; they exist in the universe forever. We have done our best to capture that energy in the talks recounted here. As he says:

"Just because you do not see it, does not mean it doesn't exist."

God knows best. ೮ಠ

Dr. Hedieh Mirahmadi
December 25, 2005
Fenton, Michigan

Small Wisdoms

Eating in Restaurants

One of the conditions of the Sufi path used to be that the seeker was never allowed to eat in restaurants. If a homeless person were to pass by and see you eating there, his envious gaze would send negative energy to you and it ruins your spiritual progress. Even if the people at the table next to you did not have enough to eat and send that envy to you, it is harmful. Nowadays, it is so difficult to ask that of people because they are always on the go. Therefore, it is very important to always recite "In the Name of God" over your food to take away whatever negative energy may be in it. ☙

The Secret to the Guide's Anger

Fellow devotees in the spiritual path should not correct one another or offend each other because it affects the heart. Every one is very sensitive and usually there is no benefit to trying to change someone. The Guide, on the other hand, has spiritual reasons why he may offend a follower. For example, if the Guide says something hurtful to you, he then owes you a favor. So as a favor, he carries the burdens of your sins. Once he has done that, he can fix the relationship back by making you laugh or saying something loving to you. The ordinary person does not have this ability that is why it is better not to hurt someone else's feelings because you cannot mend the broken heart.

The most desirous character of a follower who is toward the stage of perfection, is when the Guide could curse and yell at him in front of everyone but his heart, his eyes, and his face never changes. This is the best character the Guide loves because he can use it as an example to teach others how to control their emotions and love without condition. If you do not have that character, you have to build it. Never expect that the Guide will thank you for anything. No matter what you do, it has to be wrong because he is trying to test your patience. He wants to see if you get angry or frustrated because that means you still have too much pride and/or arrogance left. ◊

Company of the Sufi Guide

It is very important to visit and spend time with the Guide because Sufism is a path to travel, not just a theory from a book. The taste of it comes from experience. It also teaches you that you are capable of so little compared to what he is doing. It makes you humble. ◊

The Miracle of Sperm

Every individual sperm has the complete genetic composition to create a human being even without the female egg. So every sperm that is released, on Judgment Day will produce a child from that man. These children will walk behind him asking for the intercession from the Prophet on his behalf. It doesn't matter whether the sperm is from marital relations or not, all sperm released will generate a child. ◊

Weightlessness

How does a ship weighing 17,000 tons float on water? Why does a dead body float but a live person sink? Because when the mass of a ship or the body of a human surrenders to the Lord, it floats. Now ships are made with mass and are balanced in order to float. They balance so they surrender to the sea. You, too if you balance your physical and spiritual body, you will float through life. Balance is achieved by increasing the weight of your spirit through worship, which counteracts the weight of your physical mass [that represents your earthly desires]. If you manage to do that, you will see your life run smoothly.

Making Decisions

When you have satisfaction in your heart and want to make a decision, meditate. The first inspiration that comes is the correct one. Or if you meditate and a thought comes that makes you warm, it's the right one. The decision that comes from meditation is correct because it comes from energy of the spirit. The ego then comes and says, "No do this"—but don't listen.

Other Peoples Opinion of You

There's nothing in this life you take with you when you die except good manners and what people think of you. If you treat people well and people think you are a good person, God will confirm it. So judge whether you are behaving well by whether people like you.

Spending Money

The light of spirituality will not open for any one who wastes money. If you save money, use it wisely and spend it in God's way. If you follow that, God will open your way to all goodness – in this life and the next.

Miracle of the Shaykh's Spirit

One student was describing how his mother used to complain to him that he must wear proper clothes to bed because the Saints may sometime visit your home at night. He never paid attention to her until one day his daughter was very sick and she told him that she saw the Shaykh in the room. He did not believe her until suddenly he saw the Shaykh appear at the edge of the bed. He was very shy because he was still in his underwear! ✑

Blood Transfusions

After Grandshaykh had surgery for his eyes and for a hernia, he became very anemic from not eating and needed a blood transfusion. At first he refused but because his family and disciples insisted, he agreed to get two pints of blood. Later he said, "All my life I spent cleaning my blood, and that blood put me back to zero. The difficulty I have carried for the past seven days due to that blood equals what I did in my whole life." So a blood transfusion does affect a person and one should be careful about the blood he or she receives. ✑

Breastfeeding and Baby Formula

When a mother gives birth, that child can still see everything from Heavens and still has its spiritual vision to witness angels and Saints. When the mother breastfeeds, her bad manners—like not making ablution before feeding or not invoking the name of God—are transferred to the innocent baby until the spiritual vision of the child is completely covered. Feeding with cow's milk is even worse because you do not know how that milk was extracted and by whom. Powdered milk is even worse yet because many of them are filled with animal cartilage and bones!

Such things cause the diseases like cancer that we see today and did not exist before. The best thing for mothers is to breastfeed, but do so with proper ablution and spiritual recitations so they can maintain the child's purity as long as possible. ☙

To Be a Witness

Chicago

Every place is like a prayer hall—whether it is in your house or your heart. "Neither the Heavens nor the Earth contain Me, but the heart of the believer can."[2] The heart is the center of information. When we were created, it contained the love of God so He sent his light and knowledge to it. So the heart contains either heavenly messages or worldly and devilish thoughts. The heart is not just flesh; it is a place where God sends Divine inspiration and should be the focus of our attention. Without brain function, a person can live, because God is still sending energy to that person. But if the heart stops—finished. God has called that soul back.

If we cannot understand or we cannot hear the Divine inspiration they are sending us, then something is wrong with our reception. Every heart gets the signal, but very few hear it because they are not worshipping God and perfecting their characters. Excessive focus on worldly desires blocks that heavenly signal. Over time, that block becomes like rust on the heart and becomes very difficult to remove. That is when the seeker comes to a Guide to help him remove that rust. But do not think the heavenly signal does not exist because you do not hear it. Instead you must ask yourself, why you cannot hear it and what you could do to receive it.

---

[2] A Prophetic Tradition mentioned by Al-Ghazali in his *Revival of the Religious Sciences* and similar to an Israelite tradition related by Ahmad in *al-Zuhd*.

To Be a Witness

Human beings are divided into three categories. The first are "Men of God"[3] those who, male or female, keep their covenants with God. They are always straightforward, good with people and waiting until the Angel of Death takes them back to the Divine Presence. These are the pious people of all faiths. They are servants of God, who are imbued with heavenly power and inspiration. They are the ones who God describes in a Sacred Tradition as ones *"who shall not fear nor shall they grieve."*[4]

The second group are the followers of Satan who never believe in God. Finally, is that middle group, which includes most of us, who one day is an obedient worshipper and is the next day heedless.

Muslims profess belief in all Prophets, including the Seal of Messengers, Prophet Muhammad ﷺ. When Prophet Muhammad ﷺ first came, he told people just to say they accept that there is only one God[5] and recite "There is no God but Allah."[6] You say it and you believe it, even though you cannot see it. After that, Muhammad ﷺ brought the testimony of faith, which is "I bear witness there is only one God, and Muhammad ﷺ is the messenger of God." So, first they were only told to denounce their idols. It is very different from the testimony of faith. He was teaching us that as long as we cannot stop worshipping our own egos as idols, we cannot "bear witness" to God's Oneness. For Sufi's, we recite that invocation "There is no God but Allah" repeatedly so we can stop

---

[3] In Arabic it is *Rijal Allah*, meaning "men of God," where "men" in the sense of anyone whose attributes are fearlessness and perseverance, i.e. spiritual firmness.
[4] Surah Yunus: 10:62.
[5] In Islam known as *Tawhid-* or the belief in the Oneness of our Lord.
[6] In Arabic it is *"la ilaha ill-Allah."*

the hidden idol worship within us and to truly accept that we must have only One object of worship—God.

When we internalize that Oneness properly, we know our testimony of faith is sincere. For the companions of the Prophet, he brought them to a state of visual certainty so their profession of faith was really a "witnessing" of God's Oneness. Yet for us, that profession is just imitation. Could you imagine if worldly judges would accept the testimony of a witness who did not actually see anything? How can we say we bear witness if we did not? So when you think about it, we do not even deserve to claim we have accepted the real testimony of faith. What do you think then about the rest of our worship?

Bilal, one of the companions of the Prophet ﷺ, exclaimed at the hands of his torturers, "*Ahad, Ahad*,"[7] because he had reached the station of vision where he could witness not only the Oneness of God, but His absolute Unique Oneness[8], which is beyond any description within creation. He had advanced beyond the station of witnessing Oneness[9], which would have been "*Wahid Wahid*," to the level above that which is witnessing God's Unique Oneness. He saw the signs of his Creator everywhere he turned.

In prayer, during the end cycle[10], Muslims send praises to God in the absentia because He is not "present." Yet the praising of Prophet Muhammad ﷺ is in present tense. So there is clearly a distinction. God is mentioned in the absentia because we cannot

---

[7] *Ahad* is one of the Attributes of God defined as the Unique One.
[8] In Arabic known as the *Maqam al-Ahadiyya*.
[9] In Arabic known as the *Maqam al-Wahdaniyya*.
[10] In Arabic known as *at-tahiyat*.

To Be a Witness

see Him. But for Prophet ﷺ, those with vision can see him, so it is in present tense. Our blessings to the Prophet ﷺ are in present tense because Muslims communicate to God through Muhammad ﷺ. God is directing them that their approach to Him must be through the intercession of Prophet Muhammad ﷺ.

Raise yourself from the station of imitation to the station of witnessing, so you too may reach the station of witnessing God's Oneness and His Unique Oneness. You do this by accepting God's Oneness, but also knowing you cannot reach Him without the intercession of a prophet. That is why their companions reached that level of witnessing. They believed it was the Prophet who could take them to the Divine Presence. The more you believe, the more you will hear and see with heavenly power. Do not think it is difficult for your Lord. If human beings can invent infrared technology, God can't do better than them? He can make you see and hear what others cannot.

Muhammad ﷺ was described by God as the moon shining. What he gave his companions no one knows except the ones that inherited that knowledge from them. It is the hidden knowledge passed from heart to heart to God's Saints and pious servants. If you follow their guidance and be pious, they will teach you.
ಌ

Seeking a Miracle and the Power of Faith

Chicago

Over the past decade, many people have come to Shaykh Hisham asking for miracles. Whether it is a health problem or wanting to conceive a child, they come with faith in the power of Saints and love in their hearts.

One lady was telling us the story of her miracle. She was a Bosnian lady living in Colorado and her daughter-in-law was a medical doctor. They were both distraught because for ten years, she had been trying to conceive but could not have a baby. The doctors told her she would not be able to conceive. She heard about Shaykh Hisham's prayers for childbirth so she took her daughter-in-law and went to see him. It was during the Bosnian war. Shaykh Hisham made a prayer for them and he did not see them again for six months. They moved to California just to be near Shaykh because of the blessings he brought for them to conceive!

This talk was at the home of a student Shaykh talks about, who came to him with thyroid cancer. He describes for us what it really means to believe.

Unfortunately today because of excess materialism and conflict, people don't believe in miracles anymore. Despite the decrease in belief, God's ability to produce miracles never changes, especially for those who believe. Sufi Saints throughout history have used ancient prayers of the Prophet Muhammad ﷺ to cure illness and to perform what most people

Seeking a Miracle and the Power of Faith

would consider "miracles." If you ask them, they will tell you it is the disciple's faith that God will give the power of intercession to His pious servants, which brings about the miracles. So it takes three elements: God's will, the prayer of God's pious servant on behalf of a believer, and that believer's faith that God will grant the prayer, because of the request of His pious servant.

Our Grandshaykh told a wonderful story illustrating the power of faith. Once there was a small boy in a desert tribe whose whole tribe was killed. He grew up alone in the desert. God wanted to guide him but he was alone. The boy wanted to worship, but he wondered, "Who or what to worship?" This boy then looked at a bush and decided to worship it. He would pray to it every day and take care of it like it was his God. Then one day, the bush had dried in the desert heat so the wind took the bush and blew it towards the sea. The boy was running after the bush pleading "Oh my God, don't leave me!" The wind took the bush and blew it over the ocean but the boy ran after it- walking on water. It was his belief that left him without density and allowed him to float.

One of my students came to me very worried because his doctor told him he had thyroid cancer. I connected my heart to my Shaykh and he inspired me to not have this man see any more doctors. "With Prophet's blessing and God's Will, this sickness will pass. Drink ¼ cup of fresh onion juice every morning and evening for 40 days and come back to me when you are done." Glory to God, that cancer went and the student was so grateful and relieved. The Guide can do this for people who believe.

The highest level of belief for the disciple is knowing that your Guide is making this possible for you. When you believe like that, you will see even more miracles in your life. The more faith you have in your Guide, the more God opens for you of divine grace.

The power to heal would come to any believer who increased their devotion and obedience to God so that he would be described as a "Saint." Take the example in early history where the daughter of Prophet Imran said to God "Oh God, I gave an oath that whatever is in my womb, I give to you." She gave her child to Him, without conditions. When you do things with that intention, God rewards that action as worship. That means every action you do in a day may be described as worship, if you intend it to be. Nothing would be excessive. The daughter of Imran dedicating her child is an example of that, especially since she thought the child would be a boy. When she realized it was a girl, she was shy from God thinking a girl was not as good as a boy, but that girl was Mary, mother of Jesus! God is also teaching us that he honors both men and women equally when they intend to serve Him. What mother nowadays would give up her child? Who has that level of belief?

Take also the example of Mary herself, mother of Jesus. She is described as "the perfected man" in Sufi teaching because she kept her covenant with God and was profoundly pious. In this context, "man" does not mean "male," it means a descendant of Adam who honors his or her commitment of worship and obedience to God. Even Zachariah was envious of Mary's piety because God's provision for her would miraculously appear in her prayer niche. When Zachariah wanted a child, he went to her prayer niche to make a request to God. In exchange for her piety, Mary was granted one of the greatest of God's gifts, a son who would be prophet and created by His Holy Spirit.

Seeking a Miracle and the Power of Faith

God is teaching us that we must make the first step. He will accept whatever goodness we put forward in His way, especially when it is done selflessly and without recompense. If we show progress and dedication, He will honor us and open his Divine treasures. Whatever you give in His way of worship or charity, He will build for you beyond measure. If believers gave like that, unconditionally, never would we see difficulty.

Prophet Muhammad ﷺ left Makkah with only a few hundred followers and returned with 124,000. Yet, he lamented that no people harmed him greater than his own tribe. So, we must know that God's path is not without disappointment and trials, but He grants us victory in the end and sends tranquility to our hearts.

Miracles can happen when God wills and if the people have faith that Saints can intercede for them. The belief of intercession is what saves you and grants God's favors on you. God does not disappoint people when they truly believe. ☙

Meditation will Open Your Spiritual Vision

Singapore

When there is purity in the heart nothing can veil you from seeing the unseen. When there is no purity, then there is a block on your spiritual vision. Even if it is just like a "soft tissue" barrier, still your access is denied. We can only bring down this barrier with excessive worship and by constantly fighting our worldly desires. As much as you try to approach the barrier to it bring down, your Guide will also approach you and as a reward, allow you to see certain images. The more the barrier becomes transparent, the more visible these images become. As it is said in a Divine Tradition,

If you approach God one hand, He approaches one Arm. If you approach one foot, He will come to you 99 Feet. If you come to Him walking, He will come to you running."[11]

With permission of God and the Prophet Muhammad ﷺ, the Guide utilizes this secret with his devotee. So the more progress you demonstrate, the quicker you will advance.

Meditation[12] in the beginning is "blind." You cannot see anything spiritually and you get bored quickly. Satan whispers to

---

[11] As related in the Holy Tradition, "...if [My servant] draws near to Me a hand's span, I draw near to him an arm's length; if he draws near to Me an arm's length, I draw near to him a fathom's length; and if he comes to Me walking, I go to him running." Bukhari and Muslim

[12] What is known in Sufi terminology as *muraqabah*.

Meditation will Open Your Spiritual Vision

you "What is this nonsense you are doing? Just make your prayer and let's go out." Satan quickly wants to take you away from meditation with your Guide because he knows if you become vigilant, never will he be able to ride you. Meditation is the way your Guide protects you from Satan luring you into evil actions and teaches you how to perfect your character so you may approach the Divine presence. If you are able to ignore Satan's distractions and maintain your meditation practices prescribed by your Guide, God will lift that barrier between you and true spiritual vision.

What makes the meditation so important is that it is considered voluntary worship as opposed to mandatory prayers prescribed by a particular faith. A Prophetic Tradition says "one hour of contemplation of your Lord is worth seventy years of worship."[13] If one hour is worth seventy years of worship, you can see why it is so important to spiritual progress. The best formula for meditation is to decide on a particular length of time you will do it, and keep that consistently every day, even if it is only five minutes. That time spent in meditation is how we reduce the density of the barrier between us and the spiritual world. It becomes your infrared glasses to see what others cannot see.

Nowadays everybody in the world is angry. They get angry at their families, at their work, and quickly they get angry at friends even. You must know that anger is the root of all bad character traits which prevent the devotee from advancing in the spiritual path. A Prophetic Tradition says "Anger is unbelief," which means that when people are angry; there is no reasoning with them anymore. They have left their faith and trust in God, and are following their selfish desires instead. When you learn to control

---

[13] As-Sufuri.

your temper and not get angry quickly, your clarity in meditation will increase. Your Guide will not open that Divine vision to you until you control anger because otherwise you become a danger to the community. He does not want to increase your oppression on others because you will be both angry and arrogant of your spiritual advancement.

For devotees of the Naqshbandi-Haqqani Sufi Order, when they meditate, they may also see images of the Shaykh's deputies because the rank of our Guide, Shaykh Muhammad Nazim Adil al-Haqqani is so high, he has "delegated" the training of certain students to his deputies. Either way, you are maintaining the meditation practices so you can decrease the negative effect of your physical density by increasing your spiritual mass. Besides your physical weight, your worldly desires and pursuits add to your physical density and thereby decrease your ability to spiritually ascend in this life. When you can get your physical density less than water, you will float. Like when you swim; you try to decrease your density with movement. In the spiritual world, that movement is meditation. You struggle against your lower desires to maintain spiritual discipline and as a reward; your Guide will help you to float through life.

Yet at a higher stage, why does a dead body float? It floats because it has completely surrendered to its Lord. There is no more will left and the spirit has reached its ultimate ascent. If we can also surrender to God's will like that, He will open boundless Divine treasures to our heart. You will feel God's presence everywhere and it will make you "weightless" where you find peace and satisfaction in your life. Meditation will help you to reach that ultimate submission. ☙

The Power of God's Remembrance

Jakarta

This night, anyone who attended the chanting session referred to here, knows that something absolutely spectacular occurred. Even if you could not see it, the strength of the group's praising of God and the Heavenly sounds that came from the recitation of the Shaykh were unmistakable. When it was over, the Shaykh explained the significance of this session.

Praise God that there are His Saints everywhere. In this world, some pass away and others come to take their station. As God said, *"Saints are those who kept their covenant with God."*[14] Light bulbs are a human invention, but they demonstrate a good spiritual example. Light bulbs can vary widely in strength from one to another. Some are just 5 watts and can only light a baby's room while others are a spotlight that can light a stadium. In the spiritual world, the blessings that God sends on an association can either be a nightlight or an infinite spotlight. It is the same with the Saints[15]; they can either have the power of a 60 watt bulb or the strength of 2000 watts of energy and light.

In Sufi gatherings to chant the remembrance of God[16], the Heavenly emanations that descend on a group varies according to whatever God destines for that group, as well as the spiritual strength of the Guide who is conducting that session. The stronger

---

[14] Surat al-Ahzab: 33:23.

[15] In Arabic known as *Awliyaullah* but in English would be translated as Saints.

[16] In Arabic known as *dhikr*.

the Guide has connection to his Guide and all the way up the chain of transmission to the Prophet Muhammad ﷺ, the better he will be able to direct the light and divine emanations to descend upon that group.

In this particular chanting session, God dressed the group with a Heavenly manifestation never opened before. Usually these sessions have manifestations of one of two types—beauty or majesty[17]. With the blessings of our Guide, Shaykh Muhammad Nazim Adil Al-Haqqani, this association was dressed with the manifestation of majesty. Everyone's physical features in the Divine Presence were changed to resemble those of someone who had worshipped for seventy years! Saints can see that these young people here are not spiritually the same as what you see here physically. They now have a heavenly dressing on them of someone who worshipped seventy years. That majestic dress will enable the devotee to ward off 70,000 devils around them in their communities. From that light on them, it will kick of 70,000 devils even from the other people. Do not think coming to such associations are a waste of time. These are blessed meetings and you never know which one God will chose to send such kind of Divine emanations. Tonight we received this blessing because of the majesty of our Guide. It is important to keep having these kinds of ceremonies. One person from this group is enough to bring mercy and Divine power to not only Jakarta but to all of Indonesia.

When the Savior[18] comes, the people from this association will be like stars shining in the sky. Prophet Noah was building his

---

[17] The latter is known in Arabic as *Jalal* and the former is *Jamal*.
[18] Called by different names in each faith, in Islam the Savior who comes in the End of Times will be named Mahdi.

boat in the jungle for hundreds of years. People came and asked him why he was building a boat on dry land and not by the sea. They ridiculed him that if he had half a mind, he would build it on the beach. He responded that His Lord requested he build it there so he did. His community thought it was ridiculous that God would command him as such. It tells us that most people have no belief in things they cannot see. They have no faith. Without faith, you reject everything related to Heavens.

I tell you the people here will be like stars when the Savior comes, even though people may laugh thinking what we claim is nonsense. They may say doing such chanting is a waste of time. But when the Savior comes, they will be the losers and we will be the winners—just like when the flood of Noah came.

Belief in the Savior coming is as much a part of other religions as it is in Islam. Prophet Muhammad ﷺ mentioned the days when he will come and what the world will be like after he restores peace and justice back to humanity. I pray God will let us see those days and that we may be amongst those who follow him.

☙

Getting to Know the Angels

Jakarta

Shaykh Hisham's book **Angels Unveiled-a Sufi Perspective**, was translated into Indonesian and sold over 10,000 copies. It was on their best seller's list for months. Shaykh did several book signing events including this one where he recounts what prompted him to write the book and some wonderful events that happened thereafter.

In 1995, I was in Chicago at the annual book publisher's convention. There were 2000 publishers presenting their books. I attended the conference to visit the booth of my publisher and to see the work of other authors as well. Meanwhile, there was a workshop being conducted about angels and they asked me to attend. The speakers were already chosen and were all non Muslims, as well as 500 members of the audience. I was not scheduled to speak but they invited me to the panel. We never know what God plans.

The Jewish speaker presented his thesis how Judaism only acknowledges five angels. Then the Christian lady spoke about how they only believed in four angels. The Hindu and Buddhists said that neither of their faiths believed in angels at all[19]. Another speaker, who was nondenominational, spoke of her experience with angels. She told the story of how she and her children went to McDonald's after the beach and what they ordered of food, and

---

[19] None of these comments were independently verified; they were opinions of the speakers.

GETTING TO KNOW THE ANGELS

how her dog was also hungry so it was barking. Then her son put his hand on the dog and it stopped barking. The boy told his mother, "I saw a lady with wings sitting on his back, so I wanted to touch her." That's it. That was the extent of their experience with angels.

When it was my turned I explained:

Every action in this universe, in every moment of every second, is done with the help of angels. They are not only messengers to Prophets; they are an intimate part of our very existence. They are mentioned in 82 places in the Holy Quran and the Prophet Muhammad ﷺ narrated hundreds of Divine traditions relating to them. Many Muslims don't even study this knowledge, and therefore do not put any importance on the work of angels. It seems all people want to talk about is politics or devils—never wanting to talk about the beauty and majesty of angels. This is what prompted me to write the book Angels Unveiled. One classical Islamic scholar had already compiled all the Divine traditions relating to angels into one book. I used that book as a reference to authenticate why angels are such an integral part of Islam.

When I finished speaking, five people in the audience came up to me and wanted to follow the Sufi path in Islam. They knew angels were a big part of their lives, but no one had ever explained to them why. They were attracted to that reality.

Similarly, I had one man who came to me when I was in Los Angeles at an event celebrating the Prophet's birthday. He looked like someone you see in these movies about people in

Hollywood. He came up to me and said "Shaykh I have been looking everywhere for you." I was surprised. I had never seen this person before and frankly could not believe he would be looking for me. It turns out he was a famous Beverly Hills hair dresser. He recounted the story of how he went to his local spirituality bookstore and said, "Oh God, I will close my eyes and if you want me to find the truth, choose a book for me that would lead me to it." The book he chose was *Angels Unveiled*. He continued, "By reading this book, I found lots of angels of different functions which solved the puzzle of my whole life."

We must know that from every bite of food in our mouths, angels are doing the work. How do you think food has energy? It is not the chicken soup itself otherwise you could put it in the car for gasoline. It is God's command to the angels to give us a particular amount of energy in each food so we may strengthen our bodies.

Every drop of blood in the body is carried by an angel. Every cell is functioning under the command of angels and how many cells do we have? Three trillion. Each one of them is like its own country; it has security, police, army, government, subjects. How many angels do you think control three trillion cells?

"Verily everything is praising God but you are unable to hear."[20] Every element—with every atom of its composition—forms what you see in this universe. If you break down all objects into their basic chemical composition, all you are left with are atoms and their electrons and mass. What are the electrons doing around the nucleus of each atom? They are circumambulating anti-clockwise around the nucleus, just like Muslims do at the

---

[20] Surat Al-Isra, 17:44.

pilgrimage in Makkah. For atoms, they travel at the speed of light and with sophisticated scientific equipment, or the spiritual hearing of enlightened people, you can hear their praising God. The same must apply for our atoms. It must be that someone or some thing can hear the praising of our cells to our Lord Almighty.

Angels were created for the benefit of humans and this universe. A sacred tradition says "whenever people remember their Lord, angels will encompass them up to the Heavens." We cannot hear or see them but we must believe they are there. Take for example the satellite dish. Can you see the technology which allows it to project a sound and a picture from thousands of miles away? You cannot but you still believe it can do this function because you see its picture in your television. You accept there is something going on inside that dish. There are waves coming in and out of it, but normal vision cannot see it. If I told you it was actually just a sieve, you would think I was ignorant. The point is just because you cannot see something it does not mean it does not exist. If you had the spiritual vision of God's pious servants, you could see those waves.

If God can inspire humans to invent such technology, you should believe He will give even better than that to the heart of His believer. ☙

Divine Intervention

Jakarta

After this lecture, people were really frightened because they knew what Shaykh was describing was something God had done many times to past civilizations when they disobeyed His law. They were grateful to have the blessing of the Shaykh with them. To reaffirm the group's belief in the spiritual power of the Shaykh, the local representative, Hajji Mustafa, then recounted this story to the group:

> My next door neighbor came by and said "I am here to see your Shaykh. He came to my house yesterday and invited me to come see him here today." We knew Shaykh was somewhere else the day before and could not have physically gone to visit that man. Then one of our students, came to my house and said "Oh, we saw Shaykh walking down the street two days ago." Yet, the Shaykh had not even arrived to Indonesia until the day before. Saints are given the power by God to manifest in up to 12,000 different places at one time. We are so blessed to be connected to one such Saint.

A human being, whatever he reaches of high stations, still is weak. God has molded us with weakness. Our nature is that way. No one is great except God. What is the highest level one can reach in this world when just one sickness and we become nothing? All the wealth in the world cannot buy you health.

Divine Intervention

What God gave Prophet Muhammad ﷺ has no limits. He was given knowledge of before and after. *"We have given you in abundance,"*[21] God says about the river in Paradise that He gave to Muhammad ﷺ. It is not only a river in Paradise but it is infinite knowledge given to Prophet ﷺ. God also said about Muhammad ﷺ *"Didn't we give you happiness and take your sin. We raised you and everyone praised you at the highest level."*[22] Even with all that, Prophet ﷺ was humble and considered himself a weak servant. If Prophet ﷺ says this about himself, what about us? Can we then say "I am Emperor. I am a Doctor. I am a rich businessman?" In one second, God can take it away. Look outside at the stars. Imagine how small you are compared to the stars. If they were not so huge, we could not see them. But still we are arrogant. No one can speak with us or give us advice. We are stubborn and we think our minds are the best.

Everyone in the room considers they have the best mind, even a child. When God said to the sun and planets "Carry my inheritors" they refused. But man was arrogant and accepted. King Nimrod of Ancient times was given everything in this world of material possessions and power. He became so proud, he wanted to kill God. He built this huge structure and shot a bow and arrow to the sky. God sent in its way a bird. He hit the bird and blood came down. When Nimrod saw the blood, he saw himself supreme—so arrogant. Both men and women will destroy their countries for personal gain as long as it means they get to sit on the chair. Satan makes them angry. They inherit his bad manners and character.

---

[21] Surat al-Kawthar, 108:1.
[22] Surat al-Inshirah, 94:2-4.

So God sent the weakest of creatures in creation to punish Nimrod. He sent him the mosquito to show it was stronger than he. It entered from his nose and began to eat inside. Nimrod got numb inside and went so crazy he could not sleep unless his assistants would beat him over the head. They whipped him just so he would forget the pain. Nowadays, because people are behaving like Nimrod—not accepting God's authority—He is sending that weak mosquito again through this West Nile Virus. That virus is everywhere killing men, women, and children. One of our Shaykh's predictions was that God would send such kinds of sickness on humanity to clean people from evil behavior.

Scientists do not know where that mosquito comes from but Saints know. It is coming from bad character of human beings today. Just as God creates wild animals in the grave, He creates these mosquitoes to warn his servants. If Saints were to stop making prayers to save people, those mosquitoes would multiply by the millions and destroy humans. From the endless mercy God gave his prophets, which is inherited by His Saints, they are stopping those mosquitoes from invading the world.

Remember how God destroyed those who came to destroy the house of God with elephants?[23] He sent birds with small pebbles in their beaks, and these pebbles exploded on contact.

It is only the prayer of God's Saints and pious people that is stopping such destruction today. What they do for humanity no one could imagine. God said he sent Prophet Muhammad ﷺ as a mercy to humanity. In daily life, in every second, there is mercy

---

[23] An event recounted in Quran about a warring tribe that wanted to destroy the House built by Abraham which is know the Ka'bah in Makkah.

from God that is emanating from His Prophet because he is the source of mercy. Saints are asking from that mercy to delay God's wrath.

You may see the Saint sitting and drinking like an ordinary person but in spirituality, he is something completely different. What Saints carry for us, with God's permission, you cannot imagine. A day will come when the Saints will stop making prayers and they will leave things to occur as God wills. His respite is only temporary if people don't change their behavior.

If you see some behavior from one of these Saints that you don't understand, don't fight it because you will lose. Do not judge a Saint with your mind. There are wisdoms in every action he does—even up to 12,000 in a single act. Saints are hidden. They do not let people see them differently than them. But in reality they are friends of God.

Divine Offerings

Jakarta

Shaykh gave this talk was after returning from a trip to Bali, Indonesia. Though a physically beautiful place, Shaykh was not impressed with the spirit of the city. He felt its immoral decadence and wasting of food left the city without the Divine emanations felt everywhere else in Indonesia. At one point during the trip, Shaykh seemed very upset and our hosts were worried he was unhappy with the trip. We could sense his mood completely changed and it made him "fiery" so that you we were even afraid to approach him. He explained that some times there are Divine Manifestations on the Shaykh because of whatever spiritual burdens he is being asked to carry at that time. He was under the manifestation of "majesty"[24] and he advised us, if the Guide is in that state, it is better not to approach him.

After the terrible Bali bombing incident which occurred about one year after this visit, he explained to me that the Majestic manifestation we witnessed from him then was because he sensed a horrible tragedy coming to Bali and he was praying for the safety of their people. He could not say of course what the calamity was at the time, but the energy there felt heavy and he was inspired to pray for God's mercy on them.

---

[24] In Arabic known as *jalal*.

DIVINE OFFERINGS

The following lecture explains the history behind Divine offerings and why it is not recommended to lay food out on the streets as a religious ritual.

God has blessed us to believe in Him and it is from His endless favors he created us and guided us to this way. Belief in one God takes you away from idol worship. When Prophet told his companions say "There is only one God" it was to acknowledge only one true God and they must leave the worship of idols. It was taking them to worship the one God who created all of creation—humans and jinn[25].

The house of Abraham, today known as the Ka'bah for Muslims, was full of idols before Islam came. The people would offer food to their statues and anything else they thought would please them. They were worshipping the idols by giving these offerings and hoping to make them happy because they believed these statutes had to be happy with them or their lives would be difficult. You could not imagine the amount of richness in gold and jewels that they gave to these idols. Besides the jewelry, they also gave food to make them eat and be happy. This practice did not start with the Arabs; it was a custom that existed for thousands of years.

Yet, when you think about it, who needs to eat? Isn't it humans and animals that need food to survive and grow? Why would you give physical food to something that doesn't need to eat? In other words, food is an earthly element of survival, not a heavenly one. Why would a "God" want offerings of food? God

---

[25] Jinns are spiritual beings that are also on earth and have free will. They can be both destructive and supportive of man, and are made of fire and wind.

does not eat, drink and sleep. He is not of the nature and character of His creation.

In the ancient times, if someone pious gave an offering to God, a fire would come from Heavens to take it and that is how he knew it was accepted. We have many stories of that happening like the one with Cain and Abel. But slowly people started to change and instead of giving the offerings that were taken by fire or angels to be accepted by God, they started to give to idols. They even modeled the idols to look like qualities they perceived in themselves—both good and bad. In reality, they were worshipping themselves because they created these statues based on their own character.

Prophet Muhammad ﷺ told his companions "What I fear most for people is the hidden polytheism." He was referring to the human tendency to worship himself and his desires. Satan makes people believe that instead of saying "There is only one God" they should instead be saying "I am the only one God." When he convinces them to only worship themselves, you see the earthly offerings of things like cooked food because it is based on the person's own desire. You also start to see statues that look very mean or evil because that is the negative character people are seeing in themselves.

Whatever ritual offering is on the streets nowadays is eaten by dogs, cats, birds, and insects because it is a reflection of the wild character embodied in that idol. Never have you seen a human being come by to eat that food. Monotheism came to free people from such kind of belief and to direct us to the one true God. God accepts offerings from us when we feed His poor and the needy—not to throw food on the floor for wild dirty animals to come by and pick at it.

Divine Offerings

Once in the time of Moses, a pious person was praying to God that he wanted Him to eat his food. That was his prayer. God inspired his heart "I will come tonight to eat. Invite the entire village to come." That day, he prepared a huge feast and slaughtered 100 camels. The whole village was there waiting and many hours passed. Late night, a beggar-like person came by and started to eat the food. As prophets teach us, you should never refuse people because maybe one prayer from that person would be enough for God to grant His endless favors on you. Anyway, the beggar ate a lot of the food until the host came and angrily sent him away.

So disappointed, the host prayed to God the next day, crying because He did not come to his house. God responded, "I did come but you kicked me out. I am not like my creation. I do not need or eat food. So I sent one of my pious servants to eat but you refused him."

If you want to give an offering to God, help his servants. A Divine tradition says that "the food of a generous person is a cure." So whenever you are sick, it is okay to eat the food of generous people and God is most generous, never turning anyone away like that host. This is what God wants from us. When you feed or give food other than this way, you are helping Satan grow bigger in your heart and it brings darkness on yourself and those around you. Whatever you do, be a simple and charitable person.

One thing you do realize when you see these statues, is that the ugliness of the features represents our animal ego. When we see these ugly idols, we should remind ourselves not to behave with bad manners and wild character because that is what we look like when we do. If the people who worship these statues would come to believe in God, so much Divine grace and knowledge would come to them because they are sincere, simple, and open hearted people. May God guide them and us, and forgive them and us. ❦

A Burning Heart

Jakarta

This talk took place at an event known where people gather to sing holy invocations for the love of Prophet Muhammad ﷺ. At the event, the host had a lot of incense burning in honor of the ceremony. Earlier this day after the Morning Prayer, two students were talking amongst themselves that prayers in the morning were too long [they were three hours every morning, starting at 3am]. In the lecture, Shaykh addresses the complaints of the two students [though he was not physically present during their conversation] and explains the wisdom behind rigorous spiritual practices.

God said in the Holy Quran, *"Obey Allah, obey Prophet, and obey those who have authority over you."*[26] To be obedient to God is to surrender completely to His wishes. Your will must be for God and what He plans; you follow.

There are two levels for following religious laws—doing the maximum or doing the minimum. When you do the maximum, you are doing whatever you can of obligatory and voluntary worship so that you raise your level of submission to the will of God and get as close as you can to level of Saints and the traditions of prophets. The difference between that and doing the minimum is like giving charity of an ox versus a small lamb. Which is better?

---

[26] Surat an-Nisa, 4:59.

Think of two people building a house. One has a house with a bedroom and bathroom; that's it, very simple. The other has all fancy finishes like air conditioning, intercom system, electrical appliances,--everything to make it perfect. Which would you prefer?

Both types of worshippers are performing their obligations but those who do the maximum may reach perfection and the others do not. For the heavenly life, people are not very interested in perfection, but for this life, people are so worried about high quality. They do not try to build up their spirituality instead. For the dawn prayer they complain, "We are sleepy. We can't see any spiritual visions. We are depressed." Of course they think this way because Satan whispers in their ear it is better not to do more. He convinces you that there is no benefit. This is a weakness of faith.

Pious people don't complain but say, "Oh, no. I have wake up at least one hour before dawn so I can pray more." Take the example of the Prophet Muhammad ﷺ. He prayed until his feet were swollen--and that was after he was told that God forgave all his past sins. If we prayed from now until eternity just thanking God for bringing us into existence, it would not be enough to show our necessary gratitude to Him.

If you show a little progress, God will show you more. Come walking, He will come running. This is why Saints are always submitting to His will.

Nowadays people buy perfume and put it on all day to smell good. For who—one another—or for God? Which is more important? Your wife says to you, "You are smelly." She sprays cologne on you. Then she says, "Oh you are too smelly to get in the bed. Go and take a shower." There is an Arab expression one says to someone who only notices the fault of others. "Camels cannot see their own backs." They cannot smell their dead smell of wild animal characteristics which is worse than any bad smell of earth. Though we find the smell offensive, a Divine Tradition says, "The smell of a fasting person is the smell God loves most."[27]

The heart of a saint is a source of heavenly smells. It is burning with love of God and emits tremendous energy to others. He is like the Sun—a source of energy and light for others or the fuel for a spiritual fire. They are always in the process of bringing that light out and reflecting it unto their followers who are like the moon. There is a big difference between the source of light and the light reflected from it.

People gather to recite holy chants and praising on the prophets but the heavenly praising made by a Saint is much different. A normal person makes it from his tongue but the Saint makes it from his soul. A normal person recites Holy invocations, which is a good action, but it is mixed with his bad character, so the smell of it makes it so the angels don't approach. If the angels don't approach, the invocation will not bring you to Divine Presence. This does not mean the invocation is bad; it means that you mixed it with the foul smell of bad behavior. You are still rewarded for doing the worship but it does not invoke the Divine Presence you would want. No matter how much perfume you put, it won't make your Divine praising any better because you still have your wild character. What you try to do then, is make the room smell better with incense and fragrance so the angels will come and accept your Divine praising. The incense makes the smoke from the fire but without the fire, there would be no smell. Divine

---

[27] Bukhari and Muslim.

praising itself is the incense but you need the fire to fragrant the room.

There are two kinds of Divine praising—one from a living heart and one from a dead heart. The one who has a living heart has a heart full of affection and existence for the love of prophets and God. With that kind of heart, which burns like coal from his love, when Divine praising comes out of that heart, it is a fragrance that reaches the Heavens and attracts the prophets' attention. The fragrance coming from the living heart of a Saint attracts the angels and the Prophet because it is on the burning heart of someone who lives for his Prophet and dies for him. Every cell of that heart calls the name of his Prophet because he is the door to God. Obedience to Prophets is obedience to God. Love for Prophets, is love for God.

The Prophet ﷺ meant more to his companions than their parents. That is why they would say, "My parents be thy ransom, O Prophet," because everything was for him. Their entire existence was him. Nothing meant more to them and they would even sacrifice their parents' love. They lived for the love of their prophet.

A Saint who emits the fragrance of the Divine praising from his burning heart emits a heavenly smell from Prophet ﷺ himself because he is the source of incense dropping on the heart of the Saint. The bigger the Saint, the bigger the pipe is that connects him to his Prophet and the more incense that is dropped on his heart so that the fragrance reaches to Heavens. When that fragrance reaches Heavens, his Prophet comes because it is his own smell. One time a Saint in Egypt was writing poetry about his love for Prophet while his foot was in the Nile River. The river boiled from his love. Saints are like that; their love and burning hearts can emit energy and fragrance to reach vast distances. ☙

Improve Your Heavenly Reception

Malaysia

God taught us to obey Him, his Prophets, and those with authority over you. Do not disobey because what God has planned you will see. Prophet always said to make prayers for the ruler because then they will take care of you. The other authority over you is your religious authority.

In our time, everything is done with technology. The audiotape recorder is an invention so perfect it does not miss one word. What about the favors God gave to humans? Didn't He give us minds and hearts capable of recording everything? If so, then why aren't our "recorders" working anymore? They do not work because we are not near enough to God to understand Him, and Satan is playing with us. When Satan plays with us, we cannot receive our Heavenly signals and wavelengths that would guide us. According to the wavelength sent from the Divine Presence, our "recorders" should hear just as well as a machine, but something is missing and we don't receive the signal.

The signals are in the air and if we detect them, our hearts are working. When the companion of the Prophet ﷺ wanted to talk with his general, he could instruct him from thousands of miles away—from heart to heart. If we cannot communicate like that, something is wrong with our Divine receptors.

Saints can extract information through these various wavelengths. They have receivers which can pick up signals from thousands of miles away. That signal always exists and never dies. Saints never fear because for them the information is there. When they prepare to speak, they wait for a Heavenly reception; it is not a prepared speech. Every Saint will get information according to his level, the quality of the connection between him and his Guide, as well as through his chain of transmission all the way to the Divine Presence. They are like radios that receive different wavelengths depending on its technology.

The Guide will transmit the information to the students based on what Heavenly signal comes to them. It is the lineage of permission from one Guide to another which makes them "transmitters" of Divine commands. Everyone's heart can be such a receiver of information if they surrendered to their Lord's command.

With the Hubble telescope you can see a wavelength from hundreds of years ago. We have to rejuvenate our hearts to receive these signals. That is only done with obedience and sincerity.

God has put treasures in the hearts of believers, and that is why Satan chases after us. We are a target for devils because God loves us. But if we can step over them, God would love us more. Unfortunately, nowadays there is so much corruption, people don't value sincerity. Yet, when you have a Guide, he will bring back that sincerity in your heart so you can receive those Divine messages. We need a spiritual Guide from a young age so we can learn piety, don't wait until you are old. ଓ

Love is the Key

Malaysia

Our Grandshaykh and Mawlana Shaykh Nazim say the starting point of every association is, *"O ye who believe! Obey God, Obey the Messenger, and those charged with authority among you."*[28] Obedience is a good characteristic. To be obedient involves both trust and love. The companions of Prophets obeyed because they loved and believed in them. They knew he was trustworthy because all his actions were trustworthy. When you love someone, it is easy to obey him. So either you love God and obey Him; or you love Satan and obey him instead. Many of us oscillate between good and bad during our daily lives because we obey our egos, when in reality we should obey God with every breath we take. Adam listened to Satan on just one occasion and for that God threw him out of paradise to this earthly life. Imagine how many times we disobey Him, yet we do not even repent!

I was asked to address the theme of unity. One must first ask: What unity are we asking for? Until all people focus on the love of God and His commandments on us– we will never unite. *"Had God willed He could have made you (all) one nation."*[29]

For Muslims, without the guidance of Prophet Muhammad ﷺ, and for God raising the name of Muhammad ﷺ to be with His Name, we would not be Muslims. God Himself

---

[28] Surat an-Nisa, 4:59.
[29] Surat an-Nahl, 16:93.

praised His beloved servant ﷺ. What was the character of Muhammad ﷺ that God would praise him Himself?

Once I was shown a meaning of a verse of the Quran that I had previously understood in a totally different way. It is the verse about God revealing the Quran to a mountain:

"If We had sent down this Quran to a mountain..." [A mountain being the strongest object on earth] *"...surely you would see that mountain shatter."*[30]

This resembles the story in which Moses (as) asked to see God. Instead God showed Himself to the mountain, which shattered.[31] But Muhammad ﷺ (s) did not shatter. This shows us the greatness of Prophet Muhammad ﷺ. He is not like us. – The Quran was revealed to him and he was strong. God, through His angels gave him strength and revealed the Holy Quran to his heart.

To follow the prophets is our way. They are our doors, our windows and our paths of devotion and discipline. God ordered the Prophet Muhammad ﷺ to say: *"If you love God, follow me."*[32] If you follow any of the prophets, you will reach what you expect from God. This relationship of obedience is an obligation upon us up until Judgment Day. If you increase your love for His prophets,

---

[30] Surat al-Hashr, 59:21.

[31] *"And when Musa came at Our appointed time and his Lord spoke to him, he said: My Lord! show me (Thyself), so that I may look upon Thee. He said: You cannot (bear to) see Me but look at the mountain, if it remains firm in its place, then will you see Me; but when his Lord manifested His glory to the mountain He made it crumble and Musa fell down in a swoon; then when he recovered, he said: Glory be to Thee, I turn to Thee, and I am the first of the believers."* Surat al-'Araf, 7: 143

[32] Surat Ali 'Imran, 3:31.

God will guide you to His way. The prophets were created by God as a mercy to humanity, and they will always be so. Praising our Prophet ﷺ is a necessity. When a boy loves a girl, he talks about her incessantly. Why do we not feel more than that for our Prophet ﷺ and do the same? Our way to God is through the Prophets and if we keep that in our hearts we will be winners.

Yet people are not following God's commandments anymore. All believers are only concerned with materialism and politics. There is so much corruption on earth that holy people in every faith believe we must be in the End of Times. For the benefit of all humanity, we are allowed to make prayers for God to grant us the best of circumstances. The best thing that could happen now would be the appearance of the Savior.[33] We make this prayer because they will fill the earth back with the peace and justice we so desperately need.

And from God comes all success. ☙

---

[33] The Savior is known in Islamic teaching as Imam Mehdi and is expected to appear with Jesus Christ in the End of Times.

Sacred Food

Malaysia

God ordered us to obey Him, his Prophets and our rulers. Never come against your leaders, always pray for them because God knows best. This is the obedience of people with faith and trust in their Lord.

We are not just here to eat, though our host has good food. God asked us to eat for strength and to uplift ourselves in our way for seeking His love. Eating is not just physical food but for some He sends food without them even asking for it. Look at Mary, Mother of Jesus. That food in her niche, God sent to her from paradise. Whenever Zachariah went to her niche, he found provision. That heavenly provision gave her energy to reach the station of nearness to the Divine Presence. Since she was always progressing, God gave her without measure.

If we show dedication to God, He will send more to us. That food of Mary was not only providing physical sustenance, it gave her heavenly knowledge. With every bite she took, she received Divine secrets from 300 angels, each of them opening one ocean of secrets. So each bite allowed her to dive into 300 oceans of knowledge. God gave wondrous gifts to women but they ignore that and say that religion is not fair to them.

If God gave this to Mary, what do you think He is still giving His saints today? With every bite they eat, you cannot imagine how much God opens. Shaykh Nazim said that God gives believers these days, even without their worship, because we are in the Last Days and so few people still believe. Believers have those

Sacred Food

300 angels with every bite, without doing anything, but Mary had to progress for that. These angels are praising God every second on our behalves until Judgment Day. With every bite Saints eat during seclusion, God sends those angels with oceans of knowledge like He did for Mary, and without account. Their tongues are frozen from what they witness. Angels come to them and present that knowledge.

All that is asked of us is to recite, "In the Name of God, Most Gracious Most Merciful" before eating and we too can get Heavenly inspiration with our physical food. It is also important to remember not to eat with your left hand. Divine traditions say that eating with the left hand feeds the devil. God is letting Satan attack us to see if people will check their behavior and repent. May God make us like those who repent and improve. ☙

The Experience of Death

Malaysia

Science expresses the likelihood of events happening, in any given period of time, in terms of probabilities. Every human being will taste death and that taste is his inevitable destiny. It may be either a sour or a sweet experience, and we do not know the probability of how many people will experience each. Since we cannot predict whether ours will be sour or sweet, we must be careful. A Divine Tradition says that for believers, death will be as easy as removing a strand of hair from butter. It will be frictionless. For unbelievers, the soul leaves every cell of the body with punishment; and there are three trillion cells. For believers, the presence of Angel Izrail is enough to extract the soul.

Mawlana Shaykh Nazim has said:

Followers of the Naqshbandi order recite the invocation of God's name, *"Allah"* only after the invocation of *"la ilaha illallah"* which is the affirmation of God's oneness. This is because only after you accept that *Divine Oneness,* can you call upon the essence of God, by the name *Allah.* Then you can see everything in this world in its true reality.

When Prophet Muhammad ﷺ was traveling from Makkah to Medina, he stopped to hide in a cave with his companion, Abu Bakr. In that cave, he gave Abu Bakr the sacred invocation of *"Allahu, Allahu, Allahu Haq"* with which he also passed the secret of the Naqshbandi Sufi Order into his heart. The spirits of all Naqshbandis were called to be present when this happened. All the disciples were dressed with the Divine Secret of the name *Allah,* and Saints recognize them by that heavenly dress. It is because of that divine dressing, Naqshbandis are authorized to chant the word *Allah* in their invocations.

The light of God's Name, *Allah*, is increasing exponentially every second. Only by giving your pledge to follow the teaching of the Naqshbandi Guide, which means doing all your supererogatory and obligatory prayers, as well as your daily invocations, can they pass this light to you. You must complete those obligations everyday and that light will constantly increase. When the Guide receives authorization to pass that light to you, you will feel its heavenly emanations and the satisfaction it brings to your heart.

When a Naqshbandi devotee dies, his light comes out from him easily. Angel Izrail stretches out what looks like a hand and on it is written *Allah* in light! When the soul of the Naqshbandi sees that light, it realizes he or she is returning to the Ocean of Power[34] in the Divine Presence. With immense love, the light of his body will in one second like a magnet, join that Light - reuniting with its origin in the Divine Presence.

This is not a probability, it is a certainty. For other believers death will be like removing a hair from butter, but the soul of a Naqshbandi will leave the body merely by following the light of the name *Allah* to the Ocean of Power.

We must do our best not to be lazy about doing our obligations of prayer, daily meditations and invocations. This is the least we can do to show our gratitude for being a Naqshbandi. You must be a thankful servant for this grant and not be lazy for prayers. ✣

---

[34] *Bahr al-Qudra* in Arabic.

The Sickness of Material Life and Its Cure

Malaysia

The following talk was given at the house of a very prestigious family in Malaysia. Unfortunately, the host and her family were suffering many illnesses that were untreatable by medical doctors. Every trip to Malaysia, we visit this family and Shaykh prays for their improved health. Before we got to this event, however, one of the students told us the story of when Shaykh Hisham first met a lady named Mina.

Mina was also the daughter of a very illustrious Malay family of politicians. She had sought every medical treatment in the world to cure her back pain, but all without success. Fortunately for Mina, her story is one of the most extraordinary miracles the Shaykh has ever performed. When Mina first met Shaykh Hisham in 1992, she was bedridden at least 12 hours a day for 14 years. She had a metal plate in her back and could barely even walk. She was supposed to go for yet another back surgery but Shaykh Hisham said not to and instead told her to read a special prayer of praises for Prophet Muhammad ﷺ given to him by Grandshaykh Abd Allah Daghestani. He recited the invocation over her back while she lied on her stomach. After reciting it, he pounded the cane into the floor and said, "I command this sickness to leave your body through the floor of this house and into the earth." She slept after this and by the time she woke her years of agony had passed without surgery.

The Sickness of Material Life and Its Cure

Shaykh explains to both families in this talk why illness is not always what it seems to be and how all our choices in life have consequences.

In this life, whether you are rich and eating at a fancy table, or poor and eating on the floor, as long as you are sincere, both are the same to God. Sincerity is what is important. Without sincerity, either rich or poor can face difficulty. God loves a rich person who is thankful more than a poor one who is just a worshipper, because to be a rich person thanking God and giving charity is more difficult on the ego. It is also important to be humble. A short, low-rise building does not collapse as easily in life's "earthquakes."

I have students whose families come from a long line of high ranking government posts. The reason many of their family members are sick is because of an accumulation of burdens on them as politicians. When you are in government, the burdens of your society become your responsibility in front of God. For every person that is hungry or homeless, that burden will fall on the leader and his officials. As a result, the close relatives get sick because of this burden or curse, which follows them.

God Willing[35], He will purify all of us in this life instead of suffering the punishment of the grave and our Prophet ﷺ will appear before we take our last breath. That is our real testimony of faith[36], because at that time we will witness our Prophet ﷺ as a

---

[35] In Arabic this expression is said *Insha-Allah*.
[36] In Arabic known as *Shahada*.

In the Shadow of Saints

reality. People connected to Saints may experience more cleansing in this life than regular people so that they avoid the punishment in the grave, which is 70,000 times worse.

When you take allegiance to a Guide[37], you take a pledge to do a forty day seclusion before you die so that you will not have to suffer that punishment in the grave. If you learn at an early age to take worldly desires from your focus, God will grant the spiritual reality He holds in trust for you. The Guide would be allowed to open every thing to you.

If a rich person got sick, he would give away all his wealth for the return of his health. It is better to give in charity before that happens. The respect shown to saints is sufficient charity because it affects them and makes them happy – it is called a thankful servant[38]. ☙

---

[37] In Arabic known as *Bay'at*.
[38] In Arabic known as *ghaniyin shakir*.

Importance of Prayer

According to one school of thought in Islam, for a Friday congregational prayer[39] to be valid it must be the only one in the city. If there is more than one in any given city, that congregational prayer is not valid so you must pray the noon prayer[40] as well. The lesser rule in another school of thought is that if there is more than one congregational prayer in a place, the one that finishes first is accepted. Since you do not know which finished first, you must still pray the noon prayer as well.

The Prophet Muhammad ﷺ said that prayer is the cornerstone of Islam. "Between unbelief[41] and faith[42], is only prayer." God has made the prayers an obligation on Muslims and expects that we all teach that and insist on it.

Prayer contains all five pillars of Islam within it (testimony of faith, prayer, charity[43], fasting, Hajj). In the sitting between cycles of prayer[44], you recite the testimony of faith. The second pillar is the prayer[45] itself. The third pillar, charity is represented by the fact that you stop work to pray and worship, which is charity. Fasting is represented because you cannot eat or drink

---

[39] In Arabic known as *Jumu'ah*.
[40] In Arabic known as *Dhuhr*.
[41] In Arabic known as *kufr*.
[42] In Arabic known as *Iman*.
[43] In Arabic known as *zakat*.
[44] In Arabic known as *at-tahiyat*.
[45] In Arabic known as *salat*.

during the prayer. And finally, turning your face towards Kaʿbah during the prayer represents the pilgrimage, Hajj. ✥

Showing the Sweet Side of Islam

Malaysia

The following is a summary from an interview with Shaykh Hisham conducted by one of the leading publications in Malaysia. The topic of discussion was the current problem in Malaysia with "Black Magic Cults" attracting their children, especially Muslims. Shaykh Hisham explains to the reporter the approach he uses in the US to address such problems.

In the US, there is a broad freedom of beliefs so ideologies vary—including interpretations of Islam. A lot of cults have emerged in recent years so the Muslim community has been affected as well. I see many young people who are attracted to such things.

In the US we have adopted a methodology used by other rehabilitations centers for dealing with troubled adults and youth. We established retreat centers that are not religious centers, but that we run under religious and moral values. The best success we have had in those centers has been using converts to counsel the Muslim visitors. The youth with problems in cults, who would normally refuse to go to a Muslim center or mosque and instead go to a Hindu or Buddhist temple, come to our "retreat centers."

After months of uplifting them and teaching them spirituality, they turn their lives around and enjoy healthy relationships. Problems in the US with black magic and cults happen because they are exposed to so many beliefs, but we see the same is happening here in Malaysia even though it is a Muslim country. Devil worshipping is still influencing the youth and most likely that is because of what they see demonstrated on satellite television.

We offer them a solution through spirituality. We opened a centre to treat kids who run away from their faith. In the beginning, adults were surprised at its popularity. They thought religion had no spirituality and was only ritual obligations. Today we are lacking the cornerstone of our faith, which is the building of spirituality—everyone instead is running after materialistic life. Everything is about money. People pray their prayers and run back to worldly pursuits.

For us to bring back the lost youth, instead of fighting them, we need to discuss with them and not punish or isolate them. There are thousands of ways to bring them back. You should not confront them head on; you must engage them in their daily life. We involve ourselves in their daily lives. I cook for them; we talk and spend quality time together. Eventually, they realize on their own that they were being cheated by these cults.

Q - But a lot of these kids that are attracted to the cults are coming from Muslim schools, why?

A - That depends on what they were shown of Islam. Unfortunately some of our scholars don't present a balanced approach. Some religious teachers who are born Muslim are too tough. They think they can teach Islam to youth by raising a stick and shouting, sometimes even beating them if they do not understand or accept. Nowadays kids will not tolerate that any more. So if a student is only exposed to a strict, brutal religion – he runs away.

You shouldn't frighten young people into religion; you must present it sweetly. Our scholars and teachers do not choose the right approach. He does not use the kind, sweet words used by satanic cults groups to lure the youth, so we end up losing the kids.

We must use mercy on students, not punishment or anger. In the US, there are very strict laws against physical abuse of children. In the rest of the world, many kids are tortured and abused, creating rejection and rebellion in the child.

A very well known family here in Kuala Lumpur had a child in religious school, but now at thirty he is turning to devil worship. Always in his life, he was forced towards religion. That brings rebellion either as teenager or it will come out later in life.

Many converts to Islam become strong believers. They travel abroad to learn Arabic and Islam, then return to the US and either teach or lead Muslim organizations. Some of them make very good teachers of youth because they understand the difficulty faced by American teenagers. The kids like them and respond well to them so we often use them with the young groups for counseling and to teach them Islamic spirituality.

Q - If you were brought up in a strict fashion as you describe, what made you decide to use this method with the youth?

A – I studied in American University of Beirut, but was raised conservatively. In our home, there was only Islamic teaching so I had no exposure to such dangerous influences of devils and cults. When I went to Belgium in 1967, it was then that I saw how many Muslim kids were abandoning their Islam just out of frustration. It was then that it became important to me to use a better way. Also, my teachers of Islamic spirituality, were Shaykh Daghestani and Shaykh Nazim Adil who were very kind and gentle people and who also used the "sweet side of Islam" to attract young people.

Q- You praise the government for its accomplishments but people complain about them, why?

A– A ruler can never make everyone happy. That is why our tradition is not to oppose our rulers, but to pray for him. If you fight with them, the gap of understanding and mistrust will only grow. It is important as a society to hold tight together and remain strong. The society and its government should support each other and reach a compromise. ✥

You Have a Covenant

Washington DC

Before this talk, one new visitor came to meet the Shaykh. He sat quietly in the corner and did not interact with the others. When he was introduced, this is what the Shaykh had to say to him:

> You must know your promise. Every believer took a covenant with God on the day he was created that he would perform certain actions. Anyone who does not know what his covenant is; all his actions are lies to God because he is not doing what he promised. It is very important to have a Guide who can help you discover what your covenant is, so your whole life will not be a lie. Meditation is also important because the Shaykh will inspire your heart with the actions you should do which coincide with your covenant.

It turns out this man did not believe in "Shaykhs" and could not understand why someone would need a Guide for spirituality. When Shaykh read his heart and said this to him unprompted–then gave the following talk about Judgment Day–the man took initiation with the Shaykh and is a devoted follower as of today. It turns out the man is also a scientist!

The Probability of Judgment Day

Technology and modernity has made everything for us so easy that we have become lazy; computers are even flying planes for us. A Prophetic Tradition says, "Bringing happiness to people's hearts is from faith." If you are always serious, people will run away from you. This is an important issue that we need to understand as servants of God. God has mentioned everything in holy books like the Quran. He wants it to be known to encompass every aspect of life, past, present and future. To be pious is simply to submit your will to the will of God. You surrender the self to his Lord. There's nothing else.

In Islam there is a Sacred Tradition that "everything living and not living is mentioned in the Quran but not everyone can realize it." A lawyer cannot make scientific discoveries but a scientist can. To make discoveries, a scientist will work with theories until they are proven a reality. So, when they say everything is in the Quran it means it is there regardless of whether you personally can learn it or not. It depends on your level of understanding.

Once they asked a big religious scholar to define the difference between revealed knowledge and knowledge of the unseen[46]. He said, "To us there is no difference between the two because whatever you can't understand to you is hidden that's why you think there's two. But for us everything is revealed. To you, it cannot be seen but to us, it is a reality."

---

[46] In Arabic known as *ilm al-ghayb*.

You Have a Covenant

Science is the same. When they can't discover something, they say it doesn't exist. But when it comes into their physical reality, then they believe it exists. Why? What changed? Nothing. So don't say what you don't know does not exist.

How can someone who knows nothing about a religion pick up a book and understand? You must follow a system to learn. Religious teachers know this but they don't follow it either.

If you trace human history back to Adam, it is no more than about 7,000 years. This is the most we can discover of the human race. Even in the graves of mummies, we are unable to find human skeletons more than 4,000 years old. We haven't found anything older in the human race. They claim there's one that is 50,000 years old, but there is only one. That means the period of the human race is very limited. Its not millions of years like they say, it's a limited living range. If we look at it scientifically only, and not religiously, human beings have not even reached 7,000 years of existence. On the other hand, dinosaurs go back millions of years, but what happened to them? There's not even a trace of them still in existence.

The knowledge of probabilities is a very complex science. In general terms, it is the theory that if there is a chance of something happening in this universe, no matter how minute that chance may be, then that event must occur at some point in time. It is just a matter of time—minutes, years, or eons. When dinosaurs roamed the earth, they thought themselves great, even though there was a probability of extinction. Even if the probability was small, it did exist and that extinction did happen—despite their magnificent size and strength. They disappeared from the earth completely. After them came different species of animals also never expecting to become extinct, but the probability existed and they were too rendered extinct.

This should make us realize there must also be a probability of extinction for humans. Not one by one, but the whole entire race.

If the scientific probability exists of us disappearing, we must then understand there is also a probability we will be accountable for our actions in another life. If there turns out to be no afterlife, we are safe. If there is an afterlife, what will we do? Then, we must take into account the considerations that religions warned us about and cautioned us to be careful of.

Sacred traditions explain the stories of all great civilizations before us that were rendered extinct, and how God held them accountable for their actions. They also tell us we must be aware that the same shall happen to us. Therefore, in both scientific and religious terms, the probability does exist that we will become extinct and that we will have to account for every action- good or bad, large or small.

Noah called his people to be saved from a great flood but they would not believe him. He built a boat in the jungle as an example of the science of probability within religious tradition! If you were to build a sea going vessel, you would build it on the shore, but he did not do that. He built the sea vessel on land, in the middle of a jungle, to demonstrate the probability did exist that that jungle may be flooded by water. He did not say the word probability but he was also showing "there is greater probability of my Lord saving me in the jungle with my boat than of you reaching your Lord with your immoral ways." God made that probability a reality and proved His prophet was right.

You Have a Covenant

Next, take example from the story of Moses. Neither Pharaoh nor Moses could ever think there was a probability of Moses splitting the sea in order to save his people, but God made it happen. No matter how minute the probability of them being saved by parting the sea, God made it a reality. A Sacred Verse says, *"Verily these stories are for those endued with understanding."*[47] God is teaching us by historical fact, the same lesson He taught them. Fear God and the Day in which you will be held accountable for your actions; only He can save you from evil. No civilization or race has escaped accountability.

So for the coming of Judgment Day it must be the same. For believers, it is part of their religious duty to believe in Judgment Day. For Muslims, since God mentioned it in the Holy Quran, it must happen. For unbelievers they should consider it like a scientific probability of occurrence. As long as there is a chance of it occurring between zero and one (0 and 1), that event must happen, however long it takes. If that is so, should they not prepare then for the Day of Judgment? Should we not take care of how to save ourselves on that day?

A clock will tell you that with every second that passes, we are closer to Judgment Day. Everything you look at should be a sign of that reality. That is the station of witnessing. ☙

---

[47] Surah Yusuf, 12:111.

Gaining Heavenly Technology

Washington DC

A couple of students came to the Shaykh complaining about family fights. He said to them, "There is no benefit from fighting. When someone tries to provoke you in an argument, even if it is your spouse, it is better to leave it and walk away than engage in a disagreement with them. The Prophet prohibited arguing and we teach our students that arguing brings darkness to the heart." He then gave the following two talks.

Praise is to God that He created us and gave us the honor of being believers. If He hadn't created us, never could we exist. It's a great blessing to be born in this world and it is a favor more than any other that God allowed us to be in the human race.

What God plans, you will see. What humans plan but God doesn't want, can never happen. I planned to be here at 12pm, but didn't arrive until 8.30. When we came, the road was blocked by a small tree so everyone had to turnaround. But if you looked carefully over to the side, the road really was open, so we went. It's only His Will that will happen, not ours.

People are shouting and fighting with each other, but those who God wants to gain will gain. If you are written to have something, no one can take it from you. You just have to learn to submit. If someone praises you, you are happy but if someone curses you, you are upset. The only one who is safe is the one who is deaf because he doesn't hear either. If you become deaf to your ego, you will surrender to God. If neither praising nor cursing affects you, you will be stable and balanced. Like a pine tree, always green and never changing. To save ourselves, we must be deaf and not let the ego override us. If you want everyone to praise you, then you'll be proud, like a lion. If they tell you that you're stupid like a donkey, what's the difference? They are both animals!

In the life of Prophets, how many of their own family members came against them? Yet they still extended their hands in love and forgiveness. Nowadays, if someone says one bad word to us, we all fall apart. No matter what anyone says, your heart should be with your Prophet, with holy people, and with your community to build a better future. We shouldn't pay attention to negativity.

If you really love someone, you feel him/her always close to you. Always your whole mind and heart feels as if in his or her presence. It is as if you are talking with each other a lot; or when you think about that one so much, even when they are not physically there, you can hear them talking to you . What then about someone who, God says, if you greet him, he will greet you back?

Prophet Muhammad ﷺ said that God will send his soul back to answer every greeting. A Sacred Tradition says, "Answer every greeting with something better." So if you send peace and blessings to the Prophet, what do you think he's answering back when there's no limit for him? If we don't hear him answering us back, it is us that have a defect. Where's that kind of hearing that can hear the Prophet's reply? When we send greetings, we produce a sound with sound waves. It is transmitted into the atmosphere and never dies. It goes forever. If you have a good reception, you can hear sound waves even if they are hundreds of miles away. Like with cell phones. The satellites hear the digital waves in the atmosphere, from thousands of miles away, and transmit the sounds back here to earth in seconds.

Your sound can be detected until the end of this world. The Prophet ﷺ said that with the attribute of The Hearer[48], God can enable you to hear what He likes, even if it is a million miles away. Take the example of one of the companions of the Prophet ﷺ, Umar, who could speak to his commander in battle, even though he was thousands of miles away. It is heavenly technology that must be greater than worldly technology.

Don't waste your time with television and things of no moral or spiritual benefit. Let us find our personal defects so that our ears can hear what cannot be heard—so our eyes, ears, hands and feet may reach Divine places. In a Divine Traditions God says, "When My servant approaches Me through voluntary worship, I will love him. When I love him, I will be the ears with which he hears, the eyes with which he sees, the tongue with which he speaks and the feet with which he walks."[49] Where are the people who have this? They must exist. God described them as men who kept their covenants with God. Some of them passed away, but others await death. We must find them and learn from them. ☙

---

[48] In Arabic it is *al-Samee'*.
[49] Bukhari.

All Praise and Forgiveness Belong to God

Washington DC

We should always be grateful and accept that what God has given us is the best. God said, *"If you thank Me, I give you more."*[50] Complaints are never a remedy. If you complain about your problems to others, you are only humiliating yourself. It is not accepted to humiliate yourself to anyone but God. Complaints must be only to God and that's the first level of submission. When you do that, your relief from that difficulty will also come from God because you called on Him only to solve your problems. The higher level is to make <u>no</u> complaints at all.

Today, people who are looking for spirituality or enlightenment don't understand the necessity of discipline, because their egos don't like discipline. The ego says to them, "Don't listen to those Guides." Why? Your ego doesn't want a Guide who will discipline you. How then can you accept discipline? You obey that discipline either out of love or out of toughness. Saints are of two kinds. Some show tolerance, kindness, or humor to motivate their students into obedience, but others use toughness. God mentioned both in his Sacred Tradition, but in particular He mentions the importance of fear.

God is using fear for discipline, not for punishment. He also mentions the paradises for the believers, as the loving side. That way both types of people are taught. Between these two methods people learn discipline. Like a pilot who cannot turn the

---

[50] Surah Ibrahim, 14:7.

plane more than 30 degrees or it will fall – God made it automatic for us – creating that balance between praise and fear of punishment.

For the Prophet ﷺ, his best way to show gratitude was through saying "Praise is to God"[51] in every prayer. Sufi guides also teach you to recite this in your daily devotions. You recite *Alhamdulillah* 500 times a day, for the blessings of being part of the *nation* of believers. In the Naqshbandi Sufi order, we say *Alhamdulillah* another 500 times a day for being students of Mawlana Shaykh Nazim Adil Al-Haqqani. These recitations, together with expressing the proper intention before them, teach the student the discipline of saying, "Were it not for being from the nation of believers and the follower of my Shaykh, never could I be saved." It teaches the ego humility by saying, "It is not I that is saving myself, it is them." We also pray two cycles of prayer everyday, for gratitude to God.

Sufi people are expected to both *say and do* what they believe. Scholars don't teach you to do this. They do not teach you the importance of expressing your gratitude to God everyday, forcing your ego to think about it everyday, consistently. And, if you miss doing this recitation from your Guide, you must ask God for forgiveness. The Sufi path is a discipline to follow—showing you how to reach God's door of mercy. A Divine Tradition states, "For those who are thankful for provisions, it will be everlasting"[52] Guides put great stress on expressing gratitude.

---

[51] *Alhamdulillah* in Arabic.
[52] Arabic: *Bish-shukr tadoom an-ni`am.*

All Praise and Forgiveness Belong to God

Sufism teaches what each student needs to learn and understand. For Muslims, they talk about what school of thought they follow, but what is their spiritual fountain? We follow the schools of thought because those imams were closer to the time of the Prophet, when there was less corruption and people were more pious. Imams Malik and Abu Hanifah had even met companions of the Prophet ﷺ. No one can bring what they brought of wisdom. Yet, even their ideas, how could you understand it without a teacher? Sufi saints show you the way of discipline to reach the understanding of both the rituals and spirituality of religion. They show you the path to the Divine Presence.

To take another example: we also recite the invocation of forgiveness[53] every dawn prayer. We recite it with the intention in our hearts first to ask God for forgiveness for all the sins we committed from the day we were created until today. It is also a part of the daily devotions, 500 times a day. God said, *"They will come to you [Oh Prophet] and ask forgiveness when they have been oppressors to themselves."*[54] When you ask forgiveness for the sake of your Prophet ﷺ, he will go to God on your behalf. We also do a *second* set of the invocation of forgiveness, 500 repetitions day, to protect us from the sins we are going to commit from today until the future.

The Guides know your heart and what it needs. They have traveled this path themselves, and are telling us what to do to reach our goals. This is how you quench your thirst from their spiritual fountains. Religion does not just mean going to the prayer hall and listening to a sermon. You must listen, learn, and apply the

---

[53] *Istaghfirullah* in Arabic.
[54] Surat An-Nisa, 4:64.

knowledge from the fountain of saints so you advance as a soul and spirit. You must take knowledge and put it into action if you want to progress.

If we say and we believe God will save us, He will. God likes that belief. If you believe your kids are the best, then that is the best they can be. For example, if you have employees at work, and you believe they are the best, then they are the best. You say, "Oh my Lord, I leave my affairs in Your Hands." No one can judge or plan better than God. Your duty is only to enjoin what is good and prohibit what is wrong. You can show them what is right and try to correct it, but don't stay upset in your heart. You correct them to create fear but you know they are the best that God created.

Know that everyone thinks he or she is the best. No one accepts advice, except those who try and follow a spiritual Guide. They gave their hands to a master and they learned to listen. But others, no. They only listen if they have a problem. Then, they go to a lawyer and pay to have someone tell them what to do. In worldly matters, you are willing to take advice from a lawyer. What about in spirituality? Don't you think you need a Guide to understand Holy Scripture and the path to enlightenment? Why do you agree to pay for a lawyer as a guide in worldly affairs, but you will not accept one for the heavenly life? What about your account in front of God? We need to know our problems and fix at least some of them before that Day of Judgment. We will be asked to account even for a grain of rice that we wasted.

Those who truly follow a Guide are not stubborn, but those who do not, they will never lower themselves to accept one. Both the child and the senile, thinks he is the best.

All Praise and Forgiveness Belong to God

The Quran says: *"If they keep to the straight way, We will shower them with blessings."*[55] It was explained as 'shower' because in the desert they never saw that kind of rain—this shows the eloquence of sacred texts. Never would they expect such a thing in the desert. The 'shower' referred to in this passage is a 'shower' of knowledge. How else can you get that heavenly knowledge except with discipline?

Our Grandshaykh Abd Allah Daghestani [may God sanctify his secret] in 1966 went into seclusion for one year. He came out in May, right before the war with Israel, which he had previously predicted would occur. He saw the Prophet say to him in a vision, "No need to leave your home anymore. The sincere will come to you." Previously, he would go out to see people, but after that dream he stayed home and thousands came to see him. He would speak like a gushing fountain, never repeating the same thing twice. To Mawlana Shaykh Nazim he said, "You go out and travel because you are dressed with that secret." Rarely did Shaykh Nazim stay at home because people were entering the Sufi order across the world - it is different than before. He traveled everywhere- East and West- because by seeing and learning from him, thousands would follow Sufism. This is what we are ordered to do, sitting with people and calling them to remember God. In doing so, God sends blessings. We are accepted ones by God, with our Prophet as the intercessor, and Sufi saints as our fountain.

This is the meaning of the above verse, to be 'showered' with the blessings from following the way.

---

[55] Surat Al-Jinn, 72:16. The word used here for "straight way" is *tariqa* in Arabic.

In the Shadow of Saints

A person who follows the traditions of Prophets and takes seriously the obligations set forth, his conscience should show him the right way. If he wants to watch a video his conscience will say, "Why are you wasting your time?" Always the conscience gives you the right answer, but still we do the wrong thing. That's why we ask for forgiveness 1000 times a day. This is the balance. ☙

The Miracles of Modern Day Exorcisms

For Sufi Guides, healing is a comprehensive endeavor that must consider both spiritual and physical explanations. Whenever the Guide suspects there is a serious medical condition that requires treatment and he has not been authorized by his Shaykh to cure it, he advises the person accordingly. However, a lot of the time, the "sickness" people complain about is the result of spiritual problems that medicine will not cure. For example, there is a significant problem in Southeast Asia with those who practice black magic. If they cast a spell on someone, it will affect them, regardless of whether they believe in such things or not.

God created spirits made of fire known as "Jinn." They can be either believers in God or followers of Satan, the latter of which can hurt humans. However, for someone who has taken the initiation into the Naqshbandi order, Jinn do not have permission to affect him or her, unless they have permission from the Guide. Without permission there is no way they can attack. The Shaykh may give them permission in order to correct the behavior of a devotee, to increase their faith from fear, or a variety of other reasons which they know best.

Some of the most amazing "cures" Shaykh has performed relate to such kinds of spiritual phenomena.

There was this very well known family in Malaysia who knew their house was possessed by evil spirits because at night they would hear many noises including breaking dishes. It made some of the family members physically ill and had them all scared to even live in the house. Shaykh Hisham came to the house and conducted an ancient prayer for removing evil spirits.

When it was finished, the family was instructed to order to donate the meat of seven roosters to the poor for each member of the family. Then Shaykh Hisham recited another prayer on bags of sand which they sprinkled around the perimeter of the house everyday for forty days. When it was done, the spirits were gone from the house and everyone in the house felt better.

After this event, Shaykh recounts the story of a very dangerous exorcism he performed in the US, which nearly cost him his own life.

Speaking in Tongues

I was visiting a group of murids some years ago, and they brought a woman to me who was an observant, practicing Muslim; however, they feared that someone had targeted her with black magic. She spoke French and no Arabic, yet she would go out of control and begin speaking in classical Arabic and cursing Allah and the Prophet, and saying, "I am not Muslim!" At other times she would scream, "There is no God!" The sounds she made were not human, and at times her body was violently out of her control.

May Allah bless Mawlana Shaykh Nazim and Grandshaykh Abd Allah. They taught us what to recite in such situations to repel the evil spirits that possess people. Not everything you recite will necessarily cure the patient, and what you must recite varies from one case to another. So whatever they guided me to recite at that time, I followed their instruction. I began reciting and the genie possessing her repeated back to me whatever I recited. Then I shouted, and the genie shouted back. Everyone there became very afraid, as I reached a level in the recitation where either it would burn the genie, or it would burn me. At that moment, Shaykh Nazim spiritually appeared to me and instructed, "Say this…" I spoke as Shaykh Nazim instructed and it was the genie that burned. The woman returned to her senses, and the genie left her body through her big toe. ○ʒ